Advar

"Dr. Stacy Haynes is empowering parents to hold a heart-centered space for themselves and their children through her Clinical Therapy, Radio Show, and her new book, *Powerful Peaceful Parenting*. Dr. Haynes takes parents on a journey of the most common yet pivotal areas where children and parents tend to disagree and she takes the guesswork out of parenting through her proven and practical strategies, as well as inspires parents to see the glory and light in themselves and their children. Having read a myriad of parenting books in my private practice, *Powerful Peaceful Parenting* is truly a breath of fresh air. If you want to walk away feeling optimistic and excited about your children vs. overwhelmed and discouraged, this book is a parenting must-have!"

— **Crystal V. Pizarro**, MA, LPC, NCC, CHLC, CNWC, Advanced Wellness Solutions LLC

"What a great read. The points for parents are so logical and the incorporation of scripture to assist parents with the spiritual side of parenting is a GREAT idea. As a Registered Play Therapist and a Social Worker that has worked with dozens of parents and foster parents, these suggestions and tips would be invaluable tools in setting expectations and assisting parents with the enjoyment of parenting and using different strategies to incorporate peace into the process. I will definitely use the strategies identified in the book and will recommend this one to my parents. I will include it in my Lending Library for my parents to read and incorporate into their daily lives."

— **Y. Mimi Ryans**, LCSW-C, LICSW, RPT, Owner, Lighthouse Center for Therapy & Play, LLC, Elkridge, MD

"What great technique this book has to offer parents! I have used these with my daughter and have gotten great results. Looking forward to exploring more."

— **Ana Perez-Guerrero**, MSN, RN, Advanced Nurse Practitioner, Virtua Hospital

"Dr.Haynes is a outstanding motivational speaker that has captured the hearts of so many youths and their families. Her personal desire to see our youth strive and excel in their surrounding has enhance the development of my mentoring group (Men Empowering Nations). Dr.Haynes is a blessing to this community and each family she is associated with that has a desire to change."

— **Virgil l. Carman Jr.**, President, Men Empowering Nations

"Dr. Haynes has tenderly harnessed her personal parenting experiences and blended them artfully with professional expertise, to help bring peace to simple daily activities all parents share. As one who believes that body, mind, AND spirit, intrinsically flows together, and each element must find harmony with the other for healing and peace, I especially applaud Dr. Haynes for her spiritual direction and use of scripture. Her straightforward advice is uncomplicated, practical, and clearly generates from her true center. *Powerful Peaceful Parenting, Guiding Children Changing Lives* is more than a book; it is a path to peaceful parenting for all caregivers."

— **Deborah A. Beasley**, Parent Educator and Family Behavioral Consultant, Author of *Successful Foster Care Adoption* and *Sweet Pickles, The Girl Who Would Not Speak*

"Thank you so much for helping to turn my family around. I was a mom struggling with ADHD and trying to keep my head above water with my husband and four children who are diagnosed with various disabilities. Through your gentle, empathetic approach and passion for teaching me and my husband how to communicate effectively with each other and our children, we have grown stronger as a family unit. We are actually listening and helping our children, and each other, feel valued and respected while learning how to meet each other's needs effectively."

— **Valerie Amaradio**, a Parent

"Dr. Haynes is a powerful, profound women of God with an abundant evangelical love for children. Dr. Haynes' passion toward the advancement of our children and young adults. Dr. Haynes helped me become a better father, teacher and friend (with parental boundaries) to my growing daughter. As a father in Law Enforcement, a Military Veteran who served during Operation Desert Shield Desert Storm and a member of the clergy Dr. Haynes also equipped me with an added skill set which allowed me to do away with the "Do as I say do" over protective mindset. Dr. Haynes reinforced in me parenting with passion. She reinforced plant the seed of love, affection and healthy two-way communication and give her space grow. Dr. Haynes' counseling techniques are tried and proven effective. I'm a witness."

— **Minister Mark J. Benjamin Sr.**

"This book is an amazing tool for parents. Dr. Haynes has managed to grasp some of the most difficult parenting issues and put them in a easy to read format that is applicable for parents. I especially love the self-evaluation and the prayer at the end of each chapter. This is one book I wish I had when I was raising my kids."

— **Kathy Sparano**, Gloucester County Community Church

"Reading the chapter 'Peaceful Parenting: Getting Kids Up for the Day' was amazing! Visualizing my mornings, while reading this chapter in simple black and white, was more than enlightening. As a 15-year practicing pediatrician and mother of two sons, I'm always looking for appropriate and relevant reading material on parenting. Having raised one son to age twenty and another to age seven, I've experienced what works and what doesn't in a morning routine. I give a thunderous applause to 'less conversation' and 'leaving children alone.' And yes, I agree, children should have choices. Finally, not enough can be said of 'having your own peaceful time before the day gets going.' The addition of scripture and questions at the end of the chapter lends the book to the personal affect of a journal."

— **Dr. Naomi Hill**, Advocare Pediatrics

"I'd like to take a moment and praise Dr. Stacy Haynes for the difference she has made in my family's life. I must admit when I first met with Dr. Haynes, I was at the very least skeptical. But things at home with our children were out of control and my wife and I were exhausted from all the yelling, arguing, and chaos of our everyday home life. So we decided to implement Dr. Haynes' behavioral program into our daily routine. At first it was awkward, but to my amazement it actually started working. Our children, our marriage all improved and much faster than I thought would be possible. Everyone including myself became more pleasant to be around. What I can offer you is free advice, give Dr. Haynes and her strategy a chance I'm quite confident it will also improve your quality of life with your spouse and children."

— **Philip Amaradio**, a Parent

"You have done a marvelous job of articulating and arranging how to start the day right for each child and family from the very moment its day break. Behaviors in classrooms and work places start with each families preparedness for the day ahead and with the manner with which they ease into the new day or not. This is professional information, yet simple enough for the kindergartner to understand."

— **Dr Bukola Ogunkua** MD, MPH,CPRP, LPC, Chief Clinical Officer, CGS Family Partnership, Inc.

"*Power Peaceful Parenting* addresses parenting struggles using clinically-based strategies and the often overlooked, but highly important, aspect of religion. Parents reading this book and completing the exercises will certainly develop the skills with which they can really parent powerfully and live happier, peaceful lives. Dr. Haynes offers clear recommendations and practical solutions that will guide parents on a journey of better parenting and overall well-being. This book is a great addition to any parent's library."

— **Dr.Ashley Strathren**, Strathern Associates, LLC

"I love this book! I do not have children yet, but the principles that Dr. Haynes introduces are simple yet so profound. When I do have a family I will be prepared to change my children and change our life just like the book outlines. The scriptures are on point and hit the nail on the head with every scenario. I like the way Dr. Haynes allows you to reflect on the way you parent and impart knowledge to you about making subtle changes to help change your childrens lives. A must read!"

— **Lisa Wilkinson** MSN, RN, owner of Cool Pics by Lisa

"A refreshing and novel approach to parenting, *Powerful Peaceful Parenting* is a fantastic reference to guide parents through the everyday challenges of parenting children. With a spiritual heart and mind, Dr. Stacy Haynes guides readers through practical parenting that promotes peace and love and places the parent-child relationship at the forefront. Through prompts and reflective questioning, Dr. Haynes personally connects with her audience to promote personal and unique application of her knowledge. This book will allow readers to remove the stress from parenting through simple and easily executed tips and will promote healthier, happier families overall."

— **Kristen D'Amico**, MA, LAC, Co host Parenting Tips 2 Go w/ Dr. Stacy Radio Show

"Dr. Haynes successfully blended elements of personal experience and professional clinical and research experience to create a finished product filled with evidence- based methods for successful, Godly parenting. This book is a 'must have' for any parent or professional working with a client on development of effective parenting strategies. It was an easy read, full of great advice on how to peacefully parent your children during the sometimes stressful tasks and daily activities associated with raising God's most precious gifts."

— **Shannon White**, MSW, LCSW, Life Coach/Mental Health Therapist, Kingdom Care Education & Counseling Services,LLC

Powerful Peaceful Parenting

Powerful Peaceful Parenting

Guiding Children, Changing Lives

Dr. Stacy Haynes, Ed.D., LPC

This book is dedicated to my father, Richard H. DeCosta

My happiest experiences and memories in life are with my children and I hope to pass the love of parenting on to them and to my grandchildren.

Thanks, Dad, for teaching me the simple phrase "I love you and I am proud of you" and for telling me each and every day. In this way, you taught me the power of parenting.

Powerful Peaceful Parenting

Guiding Children, Changing Lives

Dr. Stacy Haynes, Ed.D., LPC

Print ISBN: 978-1-939288-78-3

Library of Congress Control Number: 2014949252

www.ParentingTips2go.com
www.LittleHandsServices.com

Author photo courtesy of Cool Pics by lisa, www.coolpicsbylisa.com

Published by hPress,
An Imprint of Wyatt-MacKenzie

Contents

Introduction

Powerless Parenting

"I never wanted to be a parent."

I was a young adult when I heard this mother utter these words and it hit home to my very heart. I had always known, growing up, that parenting could be a struggle for many.

I made a decision that day in my heart, that I would love being a parent and that I would serve God in my parenting. It wasn't until several years later that I became a parent myself, but I still remembered those tragic words as my oath to God and to my children.

Why is there so much negativity about parenting?

I've prayed for each of my kids as they grow up and I wanted more than anything to restore joy and excitement in parenting. So many people advised me while I was pregnant with my first child, to enjoy life now, because it would all change for the worse once the children come. Why do we hold such contempt in our hearts for raising children? And yes, these were Christians that would make these negative comments about parenting.

Contrary to what some people believe, Christians struggle with raising children too. I have attended churches where their bookstores sold paddles to "discipline" children. I remember leaving a women's Bible study and watching a woman who had just prayed over our group begin to yell and scream at her child in the parking lot. Ironically, our study topic had been about love. Again, we all struggle with parenting.

Does parenting have to be so hard?

I find that many of us struggle with this question while we're in the midst of parenting. We wonder if we have the ability to help our children and to successfully navigate through the many challenges that parents face.

Does this have resonance with you? Have you lost the ability to control your children? Do you feel like you are powerless as a parent? Do you wonder if somehow, you've made parenting more complicated than it needs to be?

If you're answering "Yes," this book is for you. *Powerful Peaceful Parenting* is for the parent who's asking, "Does it really have to be this hard?" And my reply is: "No. It doesn't *have* to be. Parenting is truly what we make it."

This book is about giving parents powerful tips and strategies to change the everyday experience of family life, and to help them believe again that parenting can be one of the greatest joys in life as God intended it to be.

As both a parent and a psychologist with years of experience working with children and families, I believe in the power of parenting. And I am here to tell you that we *can* effectively help and guide our children. We can change their lives by our parenting.

Powerful Peaceful Parenting defined.

My greatest wish is for families to have peace in their homes. Everything I've written in this book is directed toward this goal. To start off, we should first take a close look at the words "powerful," "peaceful," and "parenting."

Powerful
This is about having the ability or the capacity to direct or influence the behavior of others or the course of events.

Peaceful
This is a state of being when you're free from disturbance; you're surrounded by quiet and tranquility.

Parenting
We all know this is the process of raising a child or children. In my view, parenting specifically involves the care, love, and guidance adults give to their kids.

Does this sound like something you want in your home?

Powerful Peaceful Parenting: it's about real life, not theory.

As you read this book, you may find yourself thinking, "Wow, some of these ideas are just too simplistic." You may be unconvinced as to their value. But I encourage you to overcome your skepticism and try them. Just because something is complicated doesn't necessarily mean its better. In parenting, simple is often best.

Keep in mind that this book isn't intended to be a kind of substitute for therapy. Instead, it's filled with practical and Bible-based strategies to help you change your parenting style, and to develop the power to make healthy, positive parenting decisions that can change the course of your family's life.

The powerful and peaceful advice you'll find here is supported by findings in the field of parenting research and human psychology as well as by successful parenting programs that I've studied and/or participated in. Additionally, my advice is based on the many Scriptures that support loving, thoughtful parenting; it guides us to an understanding of how we can allow God to use us to be His love in our children's lives.

God has provided so much knowledge on this subject that parents no longer have to feel powerless. Instead, they can feel strong, effective, and power*ful.* Take time in the Peaceful Parenting sections to reflect on your parenting and write down the answers to the questions. So many of us have these thoughts but have never take the time to write them down and to "make our paths straight".

I encourage you to start today on this wonderful journey toward Powerful Peaceful Parenting—one that creates friendship and unity as you provide guidance, love, and care for your children both now and in the future.

Chapter 1

Directions

What you do speaks so loudly that I cannot hear what you say.

Ralph Waldo Emerson

I find that in my work, lack of compliance is a big reason why parents come in for therapy. "How do I get my kids to listen?" they'll ask. "How do I get them to do what I tell them to do?"

I often have to tell parents that unfortunately, there's no magic pill that's going to get their child to comply all of a sudden with every direction. The good news, however, is that there *are* effective strategies you can employ to encourage your kids to listen better—and to become more compliant.

Let's start with *you*. Do you give good directions? When you tell your child to do something, is it a direction that anyone else listening to you could understand 100% of the time? Is it clear exactly what it is you want to happen?

For example, let's consider the classic parental direction of "Be good." Well, let's face it, this could mean a lot of different things. It could mean "Don't hit your sister," "Don't pull the dog's tail," "Be quiet during the movie," and any number of other positive behaviors that we want to see in our children.

I've found that even in the school environment, students will often say, "I didn't understand the directions" or "There were too many directions, and I got confused." Teachers will frequently see bad behavior developing in this kind of situation.

The bottom line? Children will often follow good directions with very little difficulty.

So . . . how do we give good directions? Here are some suggestions.

Do you have your kids' attention?

This is the crucial first step. You may need to wait until the commercial or until they're fully awake from a nap. We use this strategy in other situations, too. For example, when we want something from a server in a restaurant, we wait until he comes back to our table, is looking at us, and then we make our request.

Many parents have a hard time getting their children's attention amidst the wide range of distractions we have in our homes. So you'll need to figure out for *how long* you want to have their attention and when is the *best time* to get their attention.

For some families, the best time is first thing in the morning, or while driving in the car, as there may be fewer distractions. However, if *you're* distracted or your attention is elsewhere, I suggest that you stop what you're doing in order to focus on giving a good direction to your kids. This simple action can really cut down on frustration that can otherwise occur.

Simple directions work best.

Keep instructions simple. Sometimes, thinking it's more efficient; we give several different instructions all at once. In my experience, this often brings on disaster. Even *adults* can struggle when given more than one direction at a time.

Say you have a set of instructions for your children. A very common set is "Go upstairs, put on your pajamas, brush your teeth, and get ready for bed." While you may often get compliance with the first and last instructions, often you won't get the two in the middle.

In psychology, this particular phenomenon of listening and recalling is due to what's known as the "primary effect" and the "recency effect." When we're given a list of words to remember, we tend to recall the first word we hear (primary effect) and the last word we hear (recency effect) at a higher rate than we remember the words in the middle of the list.

Your takeaway? Be aware that if you give multiple directions at the same time, there's a good chance that the ones in the middle may not happen. Simple can be more effective.

And, as I mentioned earlier, it's not just true with children. Have you ever given your spouse a verbal "to-do" list with lots of items on it? What do you find can happen from that?

Enough said.

Be specific.

We have to state exactly what the direction is and what we would like our kids to do. Vague directions get vague results. Ensure that you're making a specific request so that you can clearly assess whether or not your child complies. This ties into the concept of "being good." As we discussed earlier, it's not a very specific term.

Does your child know *precisely* what you mean when you say, "Clean your room"? In my practice, I'll often hear kids say that their parents' version of a clean room is different from what they thought it would be. The result? Conflict. That's why I encourage parents to give specific directions, which results in greater compliance.

One common mistake parents will make is to give a direction saying what they *don't* want their children to do. For example, a parent might say, "Don't hit your brother while I'm gone." Yes, it's specific, but probably not in the way you want. The way memory works is that with this kind of direction, a child will often only fuzzily recall what a parent has said. So what will run through their mind is "What did Mom tell me? Something about my brother . . . something about hitting."

And the next thing you know, a fight has broken out.

A more effective direction would have been "play a game with your brother while I am gone." Specific and tells them what appropriate behavior would look like in our absence.

Give kids time to comply.

Often I speak to a roomful of adults. I'll ask them to introduce themselves to each other. And what happens? Many of them will wait and look around, and it's not until I ask again that they comply. It's almost human nature, this need to hear requests or directions a second time. I can honestly say even at work I've had on occasion to be asked twice to get something done. We've all been there.

So if you've found yourself feeling annoyed or frustrated with your kids when your first request doesn't result in compliance, try this simple strategy. I've found that if you wait ten to twenty seconds, then give your directions again in a pleasant tone, your chances of compliance increase significantly.

For most of us parents, time—or the lack of it—is a huge issue. Many parents feel that they just don't have the time to be cajoling or pleading with their kids. And I agree. However, we don't save time by getting frustrated and yelling when compliance doesn't happen immediately. I find that children will shut down and not comply when directions are given in a negative tone. So here is a situation where a little bit of extra patience can really pay off.

Slow down and give your child time to comply with your first request, and understand that you may have to repeat yourself.

How you say it matters too.

It's important that we be mindful of our tone and our "vibe" when we make a request or give a direction. Again, this isn't just true with kids. More than once, my husband has told me that it's how I ask that makes the difference in how he responds. So keep in mind that we are asking for compliance and that it should sound that way.

Parents ask for respect from their children and children also ask for respect. Remember the old saying that "You attract more bees with honey"? Well, we can attract compliance with a sweet tone and a polite request. Most of us don't like to be ordered around. Or we feel belittled when we are brusquely told to do something. So take a moment to think about your requests and instructions. Is there something hindering you from communicating in a tone that will increase compliance?

As a mother of two I've found that giving good directions has saved me a lot of time and energy. I will often take a step back when I notice that one of my children is having a difficult time complying and I'll see if I gave a good direction. If you're a parent of a teenager, you know that she or he will remind you of your direction and what you said *exactly* if for some reason you think they didn't comply! Remember, you get back what you give.

Peaceful Parenting

Thus says the Lord, your Redeemer, the Holy One of Israel: "I am the Lord your God, who teaches you to profit, who leads you in the way you should go. Oh that you had paid attention to my commandments! Then your peace would have been like a river, and your righteousness like the waves of the sea."

Isaiah 48:17-18

Why should we encourage our children to follow directions? What benefit is there for us when we follow directions?

____

____

____

Psalm 32:8

I will instruct you and teach you in the way you should go; I will counsel you with my eye upon you.

How should we use our directions to guide our children in the way they should go?

____

____

____

What are some *specific* instructions we can give our child that will increase compliance?

Matthew 7:12

So whatever you wish that others would do to you, do also to them, for this is the Law and the Prophets.

How would we want our children to instruct younger siblings or others? Do we want them to model how we give directions?

Deuteronomy 8:5

You should know in your heart that as a man chastens his son, so the Lord your God chastens you.

How might we use how God is directing us to direct our children?

____

____

____

❁

Dr. Stacy's Powerful Peaceful prayer

Lord, teach us parents to give directions in love and kindness that increase compliance and that will nourish our relationships with our children. Allow us parents to listen for Your correction as we begin to change the destiny of our family.

Your Powerful Peaceful prayer

____

____

____

Chapter 2

Praise

Cultivate the habit of being grateful for every good thing that comes to you, and to give thanks continuously. And because all things have contributed to your advancement, you should include all things in your gratitude.

Ralph Waldo Emerson

Many parents feel that if they punish their children, then they will get more compliance. But I am here to tell you, having worked with children and families for a long time that kids will become numb to punishment and it ruins their relationships with their parents. For discipline—*healthy* discipline—to be effective, it has to mean something to your child. So bringing them inside, or sending them to their room, really doesn't mean much if they still have their cell phones and computers to interact with friends.

The number-one way to increase compliance? Praise.

Think about it for a moment. Your partner does something nice for you, like unloading the dishwasher or complimenting you on an outfit. You say, "Thank you. I really appreciate that." Your response increases the likelihood that this behavior will happen again. Use this strategy with your children and you'll be amazed by how much their behavior changes for the better. And it's not just for kids. We do this in business settings, with performance evaluations and raises that are linked to acknowledging good performance.

We call this strategy in parenting circles and school programs "Catching them being good." We have to praise the good to see it more often. Sometimes parents will say to me, "My kids are behaving badly just to get attention." If that's the case for you, I suggest you give your children positive attention when they're behaving *well,* so they won't need the attention when they're not.

When we praise children effectively, they begin to use the same type of language and will start to praise others. This is powerful parenting when we can see our children now giving to others the one thing we all like to receive: praise.

Here are some tips to keep in mind.

It has to be immediate.

You must praise them *in the moment.* It won't do any good for you to wait until you're at Grandmother's house to boast about how wonderfully the kids have been acting. You will build ongoing improvement in compliance by praising your children each and every day. Spend at least ten minutes a day praising your child for the good things he or she is doing—when it's happening! Kids notice that you're noticing. This helps to create a positive cycle of good behavior.

Unfortunately, there are days when it may seem easier to spend a lot more than ten minutes of our time yelling and punishing our kids for misbehavior. But think how nice it would be to change behavior just by praising for mere minutes a day.

Be genuine.

Kids know when we are "pretend" praising. Try to really *feel* the praise when you give it to your child. Older children and teenagers, in particular, will be able to see if you're being a phony with your praise. So only say it when you can be genuine and really mean it.

Avoid the trap of praising everything as this will also make your praise lose its luster. After a while your child will feel that she can do no wrong. This attitude is the opposite of what you're trying to accomplish! A healthy attitude can be cultivated when praise is heartfelt. And there's an added bonus for us: praise makes *us* feel good when we give it to anyone, including to God.

Be energetic.

Have some enthusiasm in your voice as you give praise. (Yes, even if you're dealing with teenagers who are sometimes sulky and unpleasant.) My kids like to see my excitement over their good deeds. If you need inspiration, think of the energy levels you might see in an episode of *Sesame Street* or *Barney.* Really! We want even our teenagers to blush when we praise them for cleaning their room or for coming in on time.

We can change the atmosphere in our home by the mood we bring to it. By displaying an upbeat, energetic attitude when praising your children, they'll get just as excited and are likely to start praising others, too. It will soften even the hardest heart if you are full of energy and love when offering praise.

Be specific.

"You did a good job putting away your toys."

"I really like how you set the table so nicely."

"Thanks for getting your homework done on time."

Let your kids know the exact thing they did that makes you proud of them. Just like with good directions, our praise should be specific. We never want our children being uncertain as to what we are proud of or what we are praising them for. When they clearly understand, compliance levels go up as well.

We can practice being specific by changing vague phrases like "Great job being good" to "You did a great job *taking out the trash*" (or whatever the particular action is). In my practice, children will often tell me that their parents don't praise them; yet the parents will just as often say, "We tell them all the time how good they are." They are honestly bewildered by how their children are feeling.

A simply remedy is to ensure that your kids know specifically what you're praising them for.

Praise often.

Praise your child every day for something.

"Good job getting out of bed right away."

"Thanks for picking up your clothes."

"I appreciate that you texted me to let me know you'd be half an hour late getting home."

And as I mentioned earlier in this chapter, our spouses also enjoy receiving sincere praise. How would our relationships change if we gave and received praise more often? Not just during the holidays or for Valentine's Day, but if *every day* we exchanged a little compliment or two. I truly believe this would revolutionize relationships across America!

As for our relationships with our children, we as parents we have the ability to change and improve them by offering daily praise. In my own life, I am so grateful to say that there wasn't a single time in my life that I did not know my father was proud of me. He praised me every day as a child and in every conversation as an adult.

Praise is powerful. Think about it for a moment. We'll listen to anyone who offers us real and meaningful praise. Neuroscience research has shown that positive emotions help the brain to focus and be attentive. So imagine how effective it can be when we are asking our kids for compliance. Without a word of negativity we can change behavior and get children to listen.

Praise the opposite behavior.

Some of the parents with whom I work are concerned about what to praise. I advise them to think about the problem behavior they're having with their children, and to praise them each time they do the *positive opposite* of that behavior.

For example, if your child hits her brother whenever she loses a board game, make sure to praise her every time she makes it through a game without physical aggression. Praise the behavior you want to continue to see. It's an effective way to help change the behavior you *don't* want to see.

I firmly believe that praise can change behavior faster than any form of punishment. My own children have learned that Mommy rewards good behavior, and I've repeatedly seen how this has an immediate impact on their attitude about negative behavior. They've learned to think twice before behaving badly.

Many parents want to know how to discipline their children—and by "discipline," they often mean punishing them. In my work, I encourage parents to instead think more about how we can praise our kids; in this way, the need to think about punishment really diminishes.

Peaceful Parenting

Proverbs 31:26

She opens her mouth with wisdom, and the teaching of kindness is on her tongue.

What do our children anticipate when we open our mouth? Negativity or praise?

____

____

____

Proverbs 15:23

To make an apt answer is a joy to a man, and a word in season, how good it is!

What words would we use to encourage our children?

____

____

____

Galatians 6:10

So then, as we have opportunity, let us do good to everyone, and especially to those who are of the household of faith . . .

What might we have to change in our home to allow praise to be effective? Is there something holding us back from praising often and freely?

___

___

___

1 Peter 3:9

Do not repay evil for evil or reviling for reviling, but on the contrary, bless, for to this you were called, that you may obtain a blessing.

How can we handle the temptation to use negativity in our dealings with our children?

___

___

___

1 Peter 4:8

Above all, keep loving one another earnestly, since love covers a multitude of sins.

To change our children's negative behaviors, we can actively focus on the positive opposite. What behaviors do we need to focus our praise on?

____

____

____

Romans 15:2

Let each of us please his neighbor for his good, to build him up.

Proverbs 25:11

A word fitly spoken is like apples of gold in a setting of silver.

When can we find ten minutes to praise each member of our home?

____

____

____

❀

Dr. Stacy's Powerful Peaceful prayer

Lord, teach us parents to praise our children and to use kindness as our most powerful tool to change behavior.

Your Powerful Peaceful prayer

____

____

____

Chapter 3

Routines

Whatever you do, you need courage. Whatever course you decide upon, there is always someone to tell you that you are wrong. There are always difficulties arising that tempt you to believe your critics are right. To map out a course of action and follow it to an end requires some of the same courage that a soldier needs. Peace has its victories, but it takes brave men and women to win them.

Ralph Waldo Emerson

For some reason, in certain parenting circles the whole idea of routine has gotten a bad reputation. Those of us who advocate for routines in our home life may even have hesitated to admit it. I, however, am very comfortable speaking out on the value of routine. If you want your child to listen to you, get on a routine for everything. Yes, I said *everything*.

One great thing about having a routine is that it automatically reduces anxiety for children. Because they know what to expect and what to do, they feel more comfortable and then compliance is easier for them.

Many parents have kids who do well at school, but have a difficult time at home. Often this is the case because the family's home life is unstructured or even chaotic.

The school day, which lasts for six to eight hours, is clearly organized and scheduled. Especially for their younger students, teachers make sure to have a visual schedule that enables everyone to know what's coming next. Even if there are going to be different "specials" such as art or music or P.E., they're scheduled in a way that is predictable. It's all about routine.

Parents can provide similar routine at home. What should school mornings be like? What about afternoons, mealtimes, evenings, bedtime? Too, think about how you'd like weekends to be structured.

Why are so many of us afraid of routine? The number-one response of parents is "Well, I can't always know what will be happening on any given day or week." Yes, I get that; neither can I. However, for about 90% of the time I go to bed around the same time, get up and eat breakfast at the same time, and so forth . . . and so do my children. Why am I such a stickler for routine? Because I find it makes our lives both easier and better.

If you're unconvinced, it may help you to really think about the *purpose* of routine. In my experience, it makes our daily lives predictable. Our directions to our kids are familiar. It increases compliance. It helps establish peace in our homes.

Sound good? Here are some suggestions for bringing routine into your family's life.

Start with the mornings and work your way through the day.

How do we schedule morning time? What will dinner look like? Who will do what after dinner? Many of us can benefit from filling in a day-planner calendar, starting from the time we get up until the time we go to bed. Or some of us prefer using apps or programs on our computer. Whatever works for you. Track your family's chores, events, and activities for about a week and guess what?

You have your routine. And most of us can establish one, just by tracking schedules for work, school, extracurricular, leisure, and church activities.

So as a starting point, take a moment and really think about what you want your children to do each and every morning. I suggest you keep it simple and keep it the same. My kids and I follow the same routine every morning on school days; we have a different schedule on the weekends, but it's still a routine. Yes, there's flexibility—thank goodness!—but the essential morning activities are the same. The kids get up, get dressed, eat breakfast, and go to school. That's how we roll.

And here's another incentive. Wouldn't it be great to have the evenings always go smoothly like clockwork, with everyone in bed at the same time every night? You *can* make this happen—with routine.

Introduce routine slowly and with enthusiasm.

Children need to know not just the how, but also the *why* we're creating routine. Even for older teens, it really helps for parents to say something like "Why all these new plans and schedules? So we can all stop having a hard time in the morning." This makes the routine more about an overall family benefit and not about the teenager feeling like someone's pointing a finger at him.

By introducing our expectations ahead of time, and by making sure everyone knows what to do and when to do it, we're going to create a comfortable situation in which compliance will be increased.

If this seems difficult to imagine, I want you as a parent to envision all the happiness you'll feel knowing that a routine will bring heightened peace to your family.

Now get your children excited with your happy face and serene attitude!

Be realistic.

We fail when we create routines that really don't work for us. Try not to overwhelm yourself accounting for every nuance and hiccup in your schedule. Inevitably, there are going to be some variations. For example, each night of the school week may have a different activity that pushes bedtime back a bit. That's OK. You can be flexible. But the key is that once we get home, we follow the same routine: dinner, bath, bed. Compliance comes from our children understanding the game plan.

So makes sure that when you say "It's bedtime," everybody knows exactly what that means and what they should be doing. Similarly, in the morning when you say, "Get up, please, and get ready for school," nobody has to ask what to do. You'll save yourself a lot of arguing by getting the whole family on the same page, right from the beginning.

I have routines for almost every area of my life. I find peace in knowing what I have to do when I get up and I find that my children are easier to manage when they know what to do and what to expect.

For example, mornings have become less noisy and stressful. We all go about our routines. The kids have time to eat a good breakfast, and so do I. I even get to enjoy my cup of coffee. Plus, no more mad dashes to catch the school bus!

Routine is about peace for parents too.

Peaceful Parenting

1 Corinthians 14:40

But all things should be done decently and in order.

What parts of ordering "all things" are difficult for us? What might be difficult for our family?

___

___

___

Ecclesiastes 3:1-8

For everything there is a season, and a time for every matter under heaven: a time to be born, and a time to die; a time to plant, and a time to pluck up what is planted; a time to kill, and a time to heal; a time to break down, and a time to build up; a time to weep, and a time to laugh; a time to mourn, and a time to dance; a time to cast away stones, and a time to gather stones together; a time to embrace, and a time to refrain from embracing . . .

For every season in my family's life, how can we provide structure and order? Do we recognize a time in our family's life that our lack of order and routine has caused additional stress?

____

____

____

1 Corinthians 14:33

For God is not a God of confusion but of peace. As in all the churches of the saints.

Describe what would routine and structure add to our life.

___

___

___

❀

Dr. Stacy's Powerful Peaceful prayer

Lord, help us parents learn to structure our day to provide peace and order in our lives.

Your Powerful Peaceful prayer

___

___

___

Chapter 4
Conflict

Peace cannot be achieved through violence, it can only be attained through understanding.
Ralph Waldo Emerson

I hear it all the time from parents: "They're siblings—they're supposed to fight. Right?" Wrong. Children do not have to fight just because they're related.

Think about your own situation. Do your kids argue a lot? And does it seem like interactions that start out as harmless get heated really fast? Wouldn't you prefer a home life that was calm and peaceful?

I thought so.

So what is normal and what is age-appropriate? I often tell folks that we have to remember that children are not born knowing how to share and how to get along with each other. We have to teach children to share, teach them to say kind words to each other, and—bottom line—teach them to get along.

A good place to start is by simply defining what family means to you. Is family all about unkindness, mocking, selfishness? No, it should be the opposite! Now, share this definition with your children. I remind my kids each time I hear any mean-spirited teasing: "Hey guys, we are a family, and we do not tease our family members." I want them to not only recognize that the teasing is wrong but it is hurtful *because we are family.* I want my little ones to really be there for each other, both now and in the future.

In most families, many episodes of teasing occur among siblings, and parents casually accept it as normal. But if this sounds like you, I would urge you to change your thinking. Out there in the real world, how many school shootings occur each year due to children being teased? Teasing adds up to serious feelings of hurt, damaged self-esteem, and low confidence in young people. That's just one important reason why we want to teach our children to use kind words with each other.

As for physical aggression, it should not be tolerated in your home life either. There should be an immediate consequence for physical violence. As with teasing, we have to send a message that certain behavior is not accepted in our home and physical aggression is one of them.

So what does this mean for you as a parent? Yes, we have to model the behavior we want to see in our children. No teasing or being sarcastic and absolutely no spanking. (I'll discuss why spanking does more harm than good in Chapter 10.)

Teaching our children to share, to be kind, and to respect our family.

One thing I often ask the parents I work with is: "When and where did you learn to share?" For me, it's an easy question to answer, since I have a twin sister; I've been literally sharing since before I was born! Yet there are so many families in which there's never been a real discussion about sharing.

Let me give you an example from a home with teenagers. With this age group, having to share a bathroom can often lead to difficulties. And lots of arguments. But what if the family talked about this issue during a time when everybody could be calm and focused? That's the time to problem-solve and plan how to share the bathroom in order to avoid the arguments. This is where we often go wrong in our home life. We wait until after the fact—after the conflicts and the upsets—to try to discipline our kids. It's so much better to teach them ahead of time.

I encourage you as a parent to think about the stressful situations you want to avoid, and then look for the teachable moments during which you can instill concepts and values in your children in a calm, peaceful way. The big idea here is that we *can* teach our kids to share and have this *always be on our minds* instead of yelling about sharing in the moment when it's not happening.

Model the appropriate behaviors we want to see in our children.

A hard question to ask ourselves is: "Do we get along with our children?" Think about it for a moment. Do you find yourself waking up in the morning primed to disagree and argue with your child? Some of us, due to a repeating cycle of conflict that we've created in our home life, have fallen into this negative habit.

So here's a little tough love. We as adults and as parents have to be the mature ones here. We've got to take the high road and, yes, look for positive solutions to conflict. A lot of us tell our children all the time "to be the bigger person," yet we fall into the same trap when we let ourselves drift into the pattern of arguing with them.

My goal in this book is to help you create, improve, and support a healthy relationship with your kids. You can have a straight-A student who always keeps her room clean, yet who refuses to even talk to you. That's *not* a healthy relationship! In my work, I often see children who tell me they argue because that's what they see their parents do.

Our task as parents is to learn how to talk with our children—and to engage in less arguing (and less yelling!).

Get help if you need it.

Once you've identified the values you want to see in your home life, start teaching your children as soon as possible. Younger is better! Don't wait until your child is a teenager to start using words like "respect," "kindness," and "responsibility." If you need help, look for positive books, magazines, websites, television shows, church, and so on, that will support you. Talk to people you trust, respect, and admire.

In age-appropriate ways, we should be talking about respect with our infants and toddlers. We should be teaching our older kids how to get along with their younger siblings even before the little ones are born. We need to develop in our children the language we want in our home, a language of fellowship and unity.

Find solutions for the ongoing problems.

I am big on finding solutions to conflict situations. Do not let ongoing fights among your children dominate your home. Actively problem-solve to figure out viable solutions that work for everyone. In my therapy practice I work with many families whose children continually argue about TV, computers, bathrooms, clothes, toys, and just about any other item in the home.

Let's say your kids are always arguing about who gets to watch what on TV. Is the solution to simply turn it off? No. It is far better to teach our children the skills they need in order to resolve the problems they're having. As kids develop these skills, we as parents will have to intervene less and less. (Besides, we sometimes make matters worse when we add our two cents.) And you'll find more peacefulness coming into your home.

My children know that I feel strongly about being a family that deals with conflict in a positive, constructive way. My husband and I work hard at modeling a parent unit that successfully resolves conflict. We want our kids to see that we are able to be kind to one another even in the midst of disagreeing.

I've worked with so many children in my therapy practice whose only wish is that their families would stop arguing all the time. Think about that for a moment. What is the sense in being a family if there's nonstop arguing and yelling? Just like us, kids want calm and peace in their home.

Romans 12:18

If possible, so far as it depends on you, live peaceably with all.

Thinking about our family's conflict situations, what steps can we take to encourage resolution and peace?

James 4:1-4

What causes quarrels and what causes fights among you? Is it not this, that your passions are at war within you? You desire and do not have, so you murder. You covet and cannot obtain, so you fight and quarrel. You do not have, because you do not ask.

When we consider what our children argue about, or what our spouse and us argue about, what might be underlying and at the heart of the conflicts in our home?

Psalms 119:1

Blessed are those whose way is blameless, who walk in the law of the Lord! Blessed are those who keep his testimonies, who seek him with their whole heart, who also do no wrong, but walk in his ways! You have commanded your precepts to be kept diligently. Oh that my ways may be steadfast in keeping your statutes!

How can we help create an atmosphere in our home that encourages peace among family members?

____

____

____

1 Corinthians 13:4-7

Love is patient and kind; love does not envy or boast; it is not arrogant or rude. It does not insist on its own way; it is not irritable or resentful; it does not rejoice at wrongdoing, but rejoices with the truth. Love bears all things, believes all things, hopes all things, endures all things.

Does our love show through in our actions, words, and deeds? Can we disagree and still show kindness to our family members?

____

____

____

____

Dr. Stacy's Powerful Peaceful prayer

Lord, my prayer is that we parents will learn to be at peace with each other and our children, to model for others what You would have for us as families: love and peace.

Your Powerful Peaceful prayer

____

____

____

Chapter 5

Communication

Adopt the pace of nature: her secret is patience.

Ralph Waldo Emerson

As a therapist I often hear parents say, "My children just don't talk to us anymore" and "We can't seem to get them to listen." Many parents struggle with communication issues both with their little kids and their big kids. And by the time I'm working with a family in therapy, communication has usually become part of a conflict cycle.

Nobody *wants* to live in a family with frequent yelling and arguments. Nobody *wants* to start their day with conflict, or to go to bed angry with other family members. But unfortunately, this is how it is for some families.

How have we lost the ability to communicate well with our family members—and if so, how do we get it back?

These questions lend themselves to very specific solutions. It basically comes down to training. Really! Think for a minute about the workplace. Very often, managers train employees to develop both their communication skills and to learn how to effectively handle setbacks and frustrations at work.

We would not think it appropriate for managers to correct poor behavior in the workplace with yelling, screaming, and throwing temper tantrums. I believe the same is true in the home. Parents are the managers of the home. But so often, after gentler approaches fail, many of us resort to communicating by lashing out.

How does screaming or yelling make us listen more? It doesn't. After a while we'll just tune it out. I frequently hear parents say, "It only seems that they listen when I raise my voice." What's happening is that everyone is being programmed to scream, and the home becomes a site of constant shouting matches.

There *is* a better way. Here are some simple, specific steps you can take to improve your family's communication.

What are you yelling about?

In other words, what is the problem that needs to be solved? Or problems? Having them linger is not the solution. Solve the problem and you'll have less yelling. Parents often feel "Our kids are old enough to know what's expected of them, and we shouldn't have to explain it again." So the underlying problem could be that the children aren't receiving clear instructions that they really understand.

I know it's not always easy, but whenever you feel the need to yell, try to find the strength to use a calm voice instead. I find that many of us yell more when we are tired and need a break ourselves. Some parents give *themselves* a short "time-out" to regroup, so that they can come back to the situation feeling calmer. This can be a very effective technique.

Is this the right time to talk?

In a heated moment, many parents are feeling "I have to talk to you and I must be heard *now.*" This is understandable, but it's not always the best mindset.

Instead, find a time that's best for everyone to talk—especially when family members aren't still actively upset about the problem situation. Keep in mind that we adults aren't always ready to talk calmly and coolly. Sometimes we're not even in the mood to talk at all! So this may be true for your kids, too.

I suggest you take the time to figure out how your kids are in this regard. In my home, my kids have distinctly different temperaments when it comes to communication, and my husband has his own style, too, when it comes to wanting to talk and being open to talking.

Also, while giving directions and instructions is very important, kids also need us to engage with them in an honest, loving, heart-to-heart way. Try to really listen to (and be a part of) your family's conversations, and make sure the love and respect is there every day.

Are you communicating in a way that will add to conflict?

Some of us as parents storm into conversations or arguments blazing with insults, name- calling, and other negative comments which, naturally, immediately put our kids on the defensive. It's much better to come in neutral and with an objective approach if we're going to solve the problem at hand.

Do we use good manners?

So many parents complain that their children are disrespectful. And children complain that their *parents* are disrespectful. It's all about the anger that gets families to this point—but as the saying goes, a calm answer turns away wrath.

Try to be respectful at all times, even when you are disappointed by or frustrated with your child. A respectful attitude will always add value to your words and to the conversation overall.

How much time do we spend talking with our kids?

In my therapy work I've heard children say that the only time their parents talk to them is when they've done something wrong or they're in trouble. Their parents will deny it, but this is a hugely important point to consider.

Do you ask your kids how their day at school went? Do you share news from *your* day at the dinner table? Are you spending time asking deep questions of your kids? Make sure that you're not just about instructions and corrections. It's important to really get to know your kids. Talk *with* them, not *at* them. This is an especially big concern for teenagers. It's not that they don't want to talk—they want to be a part of a back-and-forth dialogue.

Believe me, I know that life can be busy and that it can be hard to find the time to talk. But just think about what your family communication could feel like when you've given yourselves time to talk, ask, discuss, laugh. As parents are we always yelling or giving instructions or are we listening and asking questions?

Try taking ten minutes a day. Maybe it means a little less time on your mobile device, maybe you need to set aside the laundry basket or the TV remote. Your kids are more important. Take a few minutes each and every day, and give good, healthy communication a try.

Peaceful Parenting

James 1:19

Know this, my beloved brothers: let every person be quick to hear, slow to speak, slow to anger . . .

Do we listen—*really* listen—before responding to our children or our spouse? Has our usual approach hurt communication at times, instead of helping?

____

____

____

____

Proverbs 15:1

A soft answer turns away wrath, but a harsh word stirs up anger.

Do we know what words will evoke anger in our children or spouse?

___

___

___

Ephesians 4:29

Let no corrupting talk come out of your mouths, but only such as is good for building up, as fits the occasion, that it may give grace to those who hear.

How can we take every opportunity to lift up our family with our words? What specifically can we say to lift each person up in our family?

___

___

___

___

Proverbs 12:18

There is one whose rash words are like sword thrusts, but the tongue of the wise brings healing.

Some words that could be spoken by our family members and by us to heal our communication problems:

____

____

____

Jeremiah 1:9

Then the Lord put out his hand and touched my mouth. And the Lord said to me, "Behold, I have put my words in your mouth."

Do we seek the Lord before speaking to our family?

____

____

____

Dr. Stacy's Powerful Peaceful prayer

Lord, I pray that we parents would seek You as we learn to use communication to heal and uplift our children. May we all realize the power in the tongue.

Your Powerful Peaceful prayer

____

____

____

Chapter 6

Chores

Nothing great was ever achieved without enthusiasm.

Ralph Waldo Emerson

Parents will often come to therapy complaining that their kids "refuse to help with chores" or "pick up after themselves." In many homes, issues about housework and chores commonly spark arguments. I remember being a child and thinking wistfully that one day, when I was a grown-up, I'd never have to do chores ever again. Boy, was I wrong.

So how do we get children to help with chores? Many parents have tried to bring in a sense of pride: "We are a family so we should keep our house clean and we should be proud of our home." Unfortunately, most children simply don't buy into this statement.

What is it about chores that bothers kids the most? Their number-one complaint: "We have to do it by ourselves." It's easy for parents to dismiss this complaint, but in my observation, children often feel like, well, a servant when we ask them to do their chores while we are doing other things. And even if we *are* doing chores at the same time, children often will perceive—rightly or wrongly—that they're doing the bulk of the work. And compliance levels start to go down.

So how do we tackle the chores? Here are some simple strategies.

Start early.

Many parents wait until their children are "big enough" to have them do chores. Then these kids will refuse, saying, "We've never had to do them before, so why now?" Some parents wait until their kids are teenagers, which can lead to major frustration and conflict as teenagers often already feel overloaded at this critical time in their lives.

What *is* a good age? When your children are toddlers. Yes, that's right. Young children can help with sorting clothes, dusting, and even have fun with the mop if we let them.

It doesn't have to be perfect.

One complaint of parents is that their child will do the chore . . . but only half do it. My response? Compliance is really our main concern. With younger children especially, the more critical we are, the less likely they'll want to complete chores as they get older.

Be patient. High standards, like other activities and skills, will come with practice.

Make it fun.

What happened to "Whistle while we work"? Chores don't have to be boring. We can find fun ways to make chores seem interesting for everyone. Music, dancing, and laughter will make the time go by quickly for everyone.

Be realistic with time.

I am not a fan of daily chores for children. Yes, things do need to be maintained daily but the idea of a "daily chore" is enough to stress out any child. Think about what needs to be done throughout the week—rather than day by day—and then set a deadline for when each chore needs to be accomplished.

Most children would rather spend an hour in one day than ten minutes every day doing a chore. To them it just sounds like less.

Make it a family event.

My kids know that we all do laundry and clean our rooms at the same time. Children are more enthusiastic when they feel that their parents are part of the process—and that means doing your chores at the same time. Maybe everyone cleans their rooms upstairs and then as a team we tackle the downstairs.

We reward ourselves when we finish.

Have a great treat ready or privilege granted immediately following chore time. This makes it fun—even for parents—to know that when we finish we will all sit down and have an ice cream! Celebrate good family fun working together to keep your home clean.

My children have grown up with chores. I grew up with chores and so did many others. We were given chores as a way to teach independent skills and responsibility. These are still important skills that young people need and can benefit from. Do take the time to teach your children to take care of their surroundings—their home—from a place of honor and respect for what you own.

Peaceful Parenting

Colossians 3:23

Whatever you do, work heartily, as for the Lord and not for men . . .

How do we view chores in our home? Is it for ourselves, for our family, and/or for God that you complete your chores?

____

____

____

Proverbs 16:3

Commit your work to the Lord, and your plans will be established.

In your efforts to maintain and keep our home as a family, do we pray for guidance?

____

____

____

2 Thessalonians 3:10

For even when we were with you, we would give you this command: If anyone is not willing to work, let him not eat.

How can we establish a family routine with chores to include everyone?

____

____

____

1 Corinthians 16:14

Let all that you do be done in love.

How can we teach our children to love our home and to do chores in a loving way? Do we model love for our home?

Ecclesiastes 3:13

Also that everyone should eat and drink and take pleasure in all his toil—this is God's gift to man.

How can we celebrate taking care of our home as a family?

Dr. Stacy's Powerful Peaceful prayer

Lord, help us parents to show our children an appreciation for our home, belongings, and self by instilling a respect for all that You have provided.

Your Powerful Peaceful prayer

____

____

____

Chapter 7

Homework

Our greatest glory is not in never failing, but in rising up every time we fail.

Ralph Waldo Emerson

If homework was to ever go away, so would most evening arguments in families. Many children's behavioral problems at home and at school are due to homework issues. In recent years, homework loads have been increasing for many students, creating a heavier demand on the time of both children and their parents.

Unfortunately, many families must now spend hours each day dealing with the mounds of homework that come home and arguing is an all too frequent by-product.

How can we make homework easier? We can't. Yes, you heard me. Homework is what it is. But it's our child's attitude about homework that makes all the difference. We have to help our children value, appreciate, and, at the very least, tolerate the simple fact that some of their school learning will happen outside of the classroom.

Sometimes parents think it's great to tell their children that they hated school too or that they also thought homework was boring. In this way, they believe, they're helping their child: "We can relate to what you're going through." Unfortunately, this stance only adds fuel to the fire.

In my clinical work, when children complain about homework, I tell them, "While I might never change how you feel about homework, I want you to get through it with the least amount of problems and arguments with your parents."

As parents, we can't make homework fun for most children. But we *can* help them get through it. Here are a few suggestions:

Create a routine for homework.

Make sure that your child knows when you expect him to have completed his homework. Have a conversation with him during which you're both calm and focused.

Many children argue about the "when" of homework rather than the "what" of homework. So ask, "What's the best time for you to do your homework?" And find a time that works within the family schedule.

Make sure your child understands the work.

Many parents will say, "My kids know how to do their homework. They just don't want to." While this is true for some children, not all of them *really* understand the work and may need extra help to get through it.

Before your children start in on their homework, ask them, "Do you understand the directions? Do you know how to complete the assignment? Is there anything I can do to help?" This kind of questioning works for both younger and older kids; teenagers too.

Be present during homework time.

Children value having parents present and available when they're doing their homework. Often, they'll get it done noticeably faster under these circumstances. If you can, try to make it happen.

Don't be overly critical when correcting.

Sometimes parents correct their kids' homework expressing disappointment or frustration, which can make children feel upset or frustrated too. As a parent, it's important to keep in mind that learning isn't about being perfect; making mistakes is part of the process. Be aware of how you come across when you're helping and correcting.

Let your children decide where they do homework.

Some kids like to do their homework at the kitchen table. Some prefer their room, or the yard, or even in a closet. (I've seen it all.) Who cares where it's done as long as it *is* done.

Many parents will insist that homework be done in a specific location, which often results in arguing. This can be a waste of valuable time. Our concern should be that homework is completed wherever the child is comfortable.

Eliminate as many distractions as possible.

Children will be distracted if distractions exist. We will say to children, "Focus and pay attention," yet we have the TV on, Grandma is talking on the phone to the neighbors, the dog is running around, etc. etc. You get the point. We really do need quiet and calm during homework time in order for it to get done.

Utilize after-school programs and study times.

Encourage children who stay after school to complete their homework during their program. This will help to eliminate the "get it done" battles. Similarly, encourage your teenagers to take advantage of study hall and other free periods at school to get their work done.

What if your child doesn't have homework?

Even if your child's school doesn't give homework, I find that kids who are given worksheets at home, along with scheduled time to read, have an easier time when, inevitably, they do receive homework. Even preschoolers can be told that something as simple as tracing their letters is "homework." You're paving the way for a strong work ethic down the road.

Have children read ten to fifteen minutes each and every day—including weekends—to help make learning a part of their routine.

Allow for "brain breaks."

Even as a working professional I find it difficult to stay focused on completing tasks for more than thirty to forty minutes. After that I take a short break before jumping right back into my workload.

The same is true for children. Our brains just need a chance to regroup before focusing again. Allow children to take breaks during homework—between five and fifteen minutes—and then have them return to the task at hand.

If it were up to me, I'd completely eliminate homework, now and forever. But I've learned to value this time with my children. I also try to make learning exciting. Even something like going to the movies or having playdates with friends can provide opportunities for learning. My children often laugh at my enthusiasm for new ideas we're exploring or new books we're reading. Good—that's what I want. I'm modeling excitement for learning.

I will never forget the moment when one of my children, who was three at the time, walked into my office, pointed to a plastic sculpture I keep on my shelf, and said, "Hey, Mom, that's a humpback whale." I simply stared at him and thought, "Wow." He had learned about whales from a book we had been reading together. It was at that point that I saw how making learning fun and interesting for kids can really pay off.

Peaceful Parenting

Colossians 3:17

And whatever you do, in word or deed, do everything in the name of the Lord Jesus, giving thanks to God the Father through Him.

What would God say about our ability to help our child with homework?

____

____

____

____

1 Thessalonians 5:13

And we urge you, brothers, admonish the idle, encourage the fainthearted, help the weak, be patient with them all.

In what areas or subjects might we need to increase our patience in order to help our child?

____

____

____

Proverbs 4:1-2

Hear, O sons, a father's instruction, and be attentive, that you may gain in sight, for I give you good precepts; do not forsake my teaching . . .

What are our children learning about schoolwork by our words or attitude toward school?

____

____

____

2 Timothy 3:16

All Scripture is breathed out by God and profitable for teaching, for reproof, for correction, and for training in righteousness . . .

What might we need to learn in order to better assist our children with their homework?

____

____

____

Dr. Stacy's Powerful Peaceful prayer

Lord, help us parents to be teachers to our children and to model patience as we help them achieve academic success.

Your Powerful Peaceful prayer

____

____

____

Chapter 8
Mornings

Live in the sunshine, swim the sea, drink the wild air.
Ralph Waldo Emerson

Not everyone is a morning person. That goes for kids, too. I often find that children and parents begin their day with conflicts and disagreement the minute their feet hit the floor. Some of the parents I see in therapy are wondering, "Why does the start of the day have to be so difficult?"

Many would love to spend the little time they have in the morning enjoying the company of their children, and have everyone get off to work and school cheerfully and happily.

The reality is that for lots of us, mornings can be hard. We're in a rush, and that in itself can make everyone immediately on edge. Personally, I'm a snooze-button kind of gal, but I've come to realize that the entire family may be affected and our whole morning thrown off by one too many clicks of the snooze button.

Have you ever taken a hard look at how mornings are often portrayed in the media and in popular culture? You come away thinking, "We're a normal family if our house is chaotic in the morning. It's normal to feel overwhelmed and stressed out by the time we reach the car. And it's normal to give a big sigh of relief waving goodbye to our kids as they run on in to school."

Wrong.

We can and should have peace in our home—even in the morning. I encourage you to make calm and peacefulness be your goal. Remind yourself of this goal when you first wake up, and this will help set the pattern for the rest of the day.

Sometimes in the evenings, I'll receive a call from a family in crisis, and I'll meet them right away. More often than not, an emergency occurred not long before they made the call. Yet when I ask the child or children what happened, nearly always they respond by saying, "Well, this morning . . ." Yet here we are at 7 PM, dealing with an emergency situation that stemmed from twelve hours ago—in the morning.

It's so important to get our mornings off to a better start so that our evenings will have a better finish. We'll discuss evening strategies in the next chapter, but right now let's talk about how you can achieve peace at the start of your day.

Try to have everything ready the night before.

In the morning, many of us are scrambling to serve breakfast, get lunches made, help our kids get their backpacks organized, check homework, and even get ourselves ready in a short amount of time.

Trying to do all this in the morning can create an overwhelming list of tasks, and can easily cause stress and frustration. Keep mornings simple: get clean, get dressed, get food, and get out the door. That's it.

Less conversation.

Many of us talk too much in the morning and by this I mean parents who give too many instructions. Think about how you would feel if you walked into work and from the minute you arrived your boss was shouting orders every few minutes. Lots of us would quickly look for other jobs!

This is how our children feel if we are talking them through every step of the morning.

Additionally, many parents take this time to remind children of chores in the evening, school expectations, weekend plans, etc., which often may cause an argument.

Save this type of discussion for later. In the meantime, only talk about what we need to in order to get everyone through the morning and out the door. With my youngest, I've learned that the best time to tell him about any change in the afternoon routine is when we're in the car on the way to school.

If you can keep to only having conversation about what the day will look like, and really limit the number of directions, you'll have a much better chance of a peaceful morning that gets everyone off to a good start.

Have a routine.

I strongly recommend that you and your kids do the same thing every morning in the same order. This helps to lessen your need for giving instructions *and* lessens your frustration. My children have had the same morning routine since they were in diapers and everyone knows what they are supposed to do.

We have a set time for when I'll remind everyone that they need to be downstairs, and I'll also always say, "We're leaving in five minutes." My kids know to finish what they're doing and get ready to go.

When your kids are little, develop a morning routine that will last through high school. Trust me, the payoffs are huge—now and in the future.

Use alarms, not people, to wake children up.

I honestly believe that many of our teenagers are expecting their mothers to be in their college dorm rooms to wake them up each morning. Why? Because Mom has been doing it since elementary school.

I say this over and over to parents: "We need to allow our young people to grow up and develop independent skills." In the situation of the morning routine, many parents have never tried alarm clocks. "They don't work," they declare. I beg to differ. Each child should be using her or his own alarm clock by middle school, when it's a good time to incorporate this important habit.

Kids feel a sense of independence and accomplishment each morning when we praise them for getting up on their own. Yes, praise them! You're encouraging them to continue with this positive behavior.

This routine allows parents to do a simple room check to see if the kids are up and about, instead of having to do the old "song and dance" of trying to get them up, which so often results in unpleasantness.

Be proactive about school clothes.

What children want to wear to school can be a big problem in families. Schools with uniforms are a blessing to parents as this eliminates the need to argue about a specific outfit. But when uniforms are not an option, I will ask families who are struggling with this issue: "Who purchases the school clothes? And what clothes are not allowed to be worn to school?"

Why is this important? Let's say we've gone shopping with our young person and he picks a really cool shirt. You buy it for him, no questions asked, and yet when he wants to wear it to school you suddenly realize that even though it's a cool shirt it's not really great for school, and you say, "No, find another shirt." And the morning argument begins.

So either have a conversation before the time of purchase, coming to agreement about when this shirt can be worn, or don't buy the shirt. Problem solved. I find this morning dilemma can happen a lot with younger children and also with—let's face it—girls especially. Whenever possible, let kids choose their clothes for school but always make sure they understand the expectations of school and their parents.

My daughter has been picking out her school clothes since preschool. These all go in her closet. However, the clothes in her dresser may not be appropriate for school, and she knows not to look there in the morning. No discussion needed.

Keep the breakfast table sacred.

I feel strongly that the breakfast table should be a place of peace and quiet. Frankly, I'm amazed by how many parents argue between themselves at the morning meal—let alone the children who are allowed to have full screaming matches at the table.

Make a family commitment to have breakfast time be a "safe zone," during which no one is allowed to argue. If someone is upset, then they can simply leave the table and get themselves together somewhere else. By the time our children become teenagers, often they no longer want to sit for breakfast and when they do they are irritable or silent anyway.

We can enjoy the silence and not press for conversation, as this may trigger conflict. Remember, our goal is peace in the morning.

Make breakfast a choice.

If possible, try to offer more than one option for breakfast, and introduce variety if you can. I know for myself I don't want to eat the same thing every day, and just because I had oatmeal a week ago, I may not be in the mood for it today. It can really help to have flexibility with food choices in the morning.

In my house, I've found that by asking about breakfast before I get down to the kitchen, I usually have better compliance. But I also try to have some quick, easy backup options as well, like protein shakes, cereal, toast, or nutrition bars if I've got a picky eater on my hands. Usually, just knowing that there are other options lends itself to less resistance and a better response rate. Again, my goal here is to keep breakfast time peaceful.

Children will eat if they are hungry. Don't let yourself get caught in a battle about what they eat first thing in the morning.

Have your own peaceful time before the day gets going.

Each morning, before my husband and kids get up, I take a little time to pray and map out my day. And I also try to have a few minutes of quiet time with my husband if possible. It's such a nice start to the day. Even just five or ten minutes of "peaceful time" can make a big difference.

Mornings are a big deal to me. Sometimes I get up really early and get my exercise in. And I just love my cup of coffee, especially when I don't have to rush through it. When things go smoothly, and everybody is off to school and work feeling good, then I know we have had a peaceful morning.

Peaceful Parenting

Job 38:12

Have you commanded the morning since your days began, and caused the dawn to know its place . . .

What power do we feel over the morning? What's keeping us from having control of our mornings?

____

____

____

Lamentations 3:22-23

The steadfast love of the Lord never ceases; his mercies never come to an end; they are new every morning; great is your faithfulness.

Do we wake up each morning with new attitudes toward our children, for our spouse, or for ourselves? Or do we continue with the same strife each day?

Psalms 143:8

Let me hear in the morning of your steadfast love,
for in you I trust. Make me know the way I should go,
for to you I lift up my soul.

Do we quiet our own hearts each morning to hear how God would have us to be today? Do we ask God for guidance and for strength to handle the challenges of each new day?

Psalms 30:5

For his anger is but for a moment, and his favor is for a lifetime. Weeping may tarry for the night, but joy comes with the morning.

Can we make joy come each morning for our family? How can we make mornings worth getting up for?

____

____

____

Dr. Stacy's Powerful Peaceful prayer

Lord, teach us parents to seek You first in the morning, to find Your mercies new each day as a way to give joy and peace to our family, and to get us all off to a good start.

Your Powerful Peaceful prayer

____

____

____

____

Chapter 9

Bedtime

Finish each day and be done with it. You have done what you could. Some blunders and absurdities no doubt crept in; forget them as soon as you can. Tomorrow is a new day. You shall begin it serenely and with too high a spirit to be encumbered with your old nonsense.

Ralph Waldo Emerson

Just as mornings can be a difficult time for the entire family, so can evenings. As I mentioned in the previous chapter, in my work I've found that many conflicts that began in the morning will erupt as full-blown arguments during this time. Too, parents will often seek therapy for a child who has major difficulties in going to bed, falling asleep, and staying asleep.

Some difficulty with bedtime depends on a child's age and can be developmentally appropriate. Mothers-to-be are often told playfully, "Get all your sleep now before the baby comes." Those of us with kids understand it, because we know that an infant will initially be up every two to three hours and will interrupt our sleep. However, it's a different situation when an eight-year-old is not sleeping though the night.

But what about older children? It is normal to be waking up during the night? The answer is yes. Whether they are in preschool, elementary school, or all the way through college age, many young people have night awakenings, are night owls, or just have a hard time falling (and staying) asleep. We're all different.

Each age and stage can have its own difficulties when it comes to bedtime. Here are some pointers on how to make evenings peaceful.

Routine, routine, routine.

By now you've heard this word from me more than once! So you won't be surprised when I urge you to establish an evening routine. I tell parents, "Even with infants, you can begin a routine that helps them to settle better." Many families find their evening schedule changing as children get older, with all kinds of sports and other extracurricular activities, but try to stick to your routine even if you need to start it a little later. Consistency is the key.

Eliminate the noise.

When I worked in a residential facility for teenage girls, we had a wonderful "lights out" policy. We would begin thirty minutes before bedtime, dimming the lights on the unit and turning down the volume on televisions, phone calls, and even our own conversations.

This helped to prepare the fifteen girls in our care to settle down for the evening without us saying a word. Each girl knew bedtime was near once those lights dimmed. Take a few minutes to consider how you prepare your home for bedtime.

Spend time with each child.

I've heard lots of parents complain about the constant demand from children to stay with them at bedtime—the little ones especially. It can become a battle when we as parents have other things that we planned to do once the children are settled in bed. If you're experiencing a lot of conflict around this, I recommend changing your plan.

Try to spend thirty to forty-five minutes at bedtime with small children. (You can reduce the time as they get older.) Set up your kids in their own rooms, and spend these bedtime moments there. In my experience it's a better strategy than having them fall asleep in the parents' bed. Once your children are asleep, you can simply slip out of the room, instead of having to carry them back to their own beds, worrying that you're going to wake them up as you do so.

Schedule your evening so that you can get chores completed, emails checked, and everything else done that might otherwise pull you away from focusing on bedtime. Have you ever noticed that children seem to sense when we're rushing through the bedtime routine just to get to other things?

In my house, I'm currently allotting at least one and a

half hours for the full nighttime routine from beginning to end.

Help prepare for the next day.

In the evening, you and your kids can start to wind down by preparing for the next day. Select and lay out school clothes, organize book bags or backpacks, make lunches, etc. This is a great way to signal "OK, now we're starting to get ready for bed."

Limit entertainment devices before bed.

The research is now making its way to the mainstream about our new technologies and their negative impact on sleep, but many of us have known for years the undesirable effect of television on children. Screen time in the evening should be limited and cut off at least an hour before bed. Our minds need time to "log off" from any and all electronic devices.

I advise parents to keep televisions, computers, and other electronics out of their kids' bedrooms. Store them elsewhere for the night. Many children aren't able to resist the temptation of these devices.

For teenagers, I suggest that you set up a charging station for their electronics somewhere else besides their bedroom. This will help to eliminate the late-night phone calls, text messaging, and gaming that often keeps teenagers up at night.

Choose late-night snacks carefully.

In addition to sugar, lots of desserts or sweet snacks often have caffeine and other ingredients that can keep kids stimulated and wide-eyed, when you want them to be feeling tired and relaxed. If this is happening in your house, I recommend keeping a log of the nights your child complains about poor sleep; observe their food intake for the evening. You may be surprised at what you see. Even so-called healthy snacks may pack a bunch of sugar that keeps your little one up until the wee hours of the morning.

Schedule your own quiet time.

Whether it's watching television, reading a good book, or having a cup of tea, make it a point to reward yourself at night with your own quiet time. I have found that having the last thirty minutes before I go to bed be all about me has allowed me to be present with everyone else the rest of the evening. I know that my time of rest and relaxation is coming and that I must work now to get to that time.

Dealing with refusal.

When kids refuse to go to bed or to stay in bed, parents will often engage in battle. This struggle frequently starts when toddlers discover how to climb out of their cribs or get out of their beds. Instead of arguing about it, I've found that this problem can easily be solved by allowing a child to be up but staying in their room.

My son was a night owl and there were plenty of

evenings when he wasn't tired at bedtime. We would allow him to stay up, but in his room—and usually by the time I was ready for bed he would be sound asleep.

Don't make this an argument. Decide to either stay with the child until she falls asleep or allow her to stay awake in her room. This is a much more effective solution than cajoling, arguing, feeling powerless, getting angry, and so on. Forcing kids to go to bed is a no-win situation. Let's try gentleness as an approach.

If they're going to stay awake, small toys, paper and pencil, and books are great items to have nearby, so children can quietly entertain themselves.

If you really want them to hop into bed and fall asleep quickly, you may want to consider finding activities that will help kids burn off extra energy, so that they'll be really tired at bedtime. Also, you can try starting the bedtime routine later in the evening.

Bedtimes in my home have always been very structured. I drew inspiration from my own childhood. I have fond memories of my mother and father always coming in to say goodnight to us kids once we were snuggled in bed.

My children benefit from this same approach and they expect that after bath, books, and songs, they will always hear the wonderful words "I love you and I am proud of you" before they drift into sleep. It can sometimes feel like a lot of work creating these evening routines, but I truly believe it's worth it in order to have all the calmness and the peace. I like how it feels when I drift off to sleep, too.

Judges 20:26

Then all the people of Israel, the whole army, went up and came to Bethel and wept. They sat there before the Lord and fasted that day until evening, and offered burnt offerings and peace offerings before the Lord.

How can we continually bring peace into our evening routine?

____

____

____

Matthew 11:28-30

Come to me, all who labor and are heavy laden, and I will give you rest. Take my yoke upon you, and learn from me, for I am gentle and lowly in heart, and you will find rest for your souls. For my yoke is easy, and my burden is light.

God would have for each of us to have rest. Finding rest also includes being gentle. How can we practice gentleness in our evening routine?

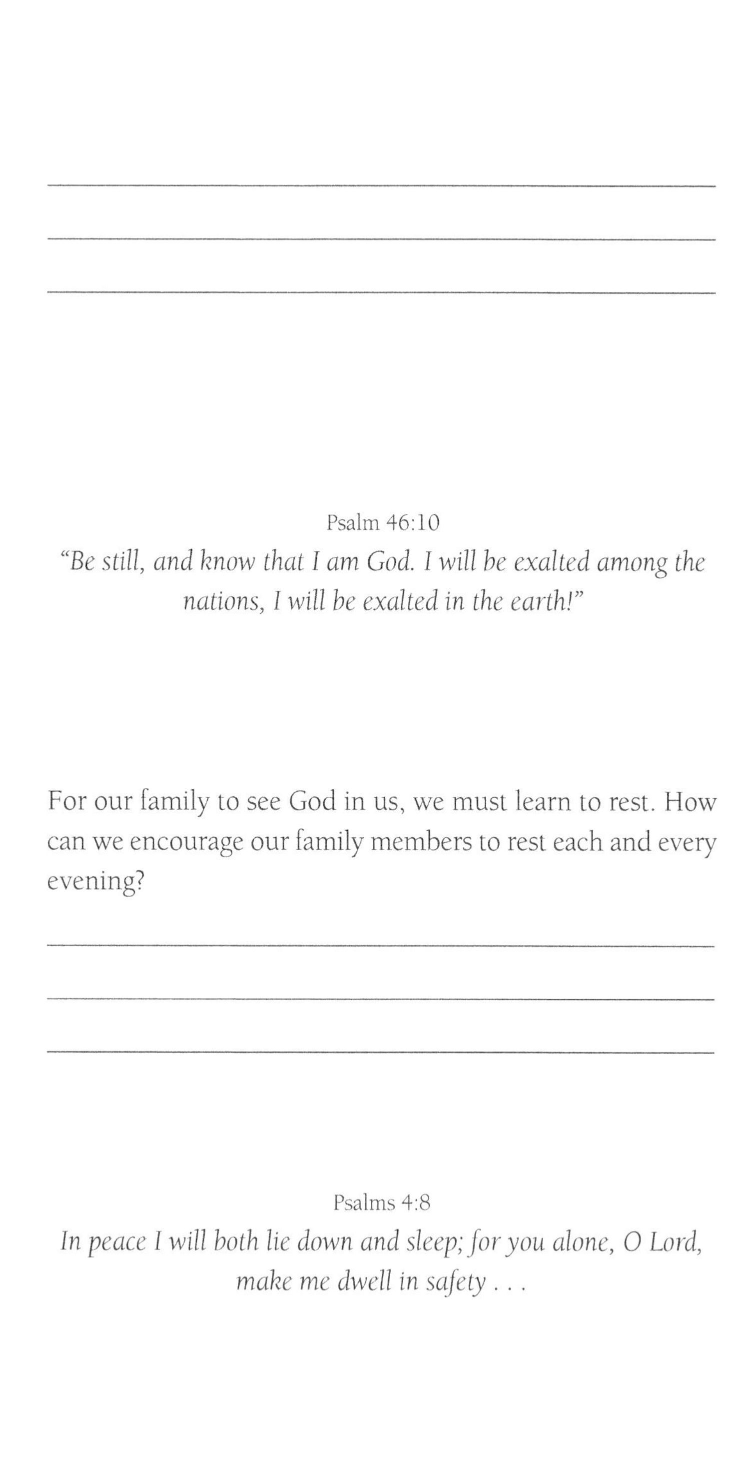

Psalm 46:10

"Be still, and know that I am God. I will be exalted among the nations, I will be exalted in the earth!"

For our family to see God in us, we must learn to rest. How can we encourage our family members to rest each and every evening?

Psalms 4:8

In peace I will both lie down and sleep; for you alone, O Lord, make me dwell in safety . . .

Are my own fears and anxiety keeping my family members or myself from sleeping restfully at night? How can we create an atmosphere of safety in our spirit?

____

____

____

Isaiah 40:28-31

Have you not known? Have you not heard? The Lord is the everlasting God, the Creator of the ends of the earth. He does not faint or grow weary; his understanding is unsearchable. He gives power to the faint, and to him who has no might he increases strength. Even youths shall faint and be weary, and young men shall fall exhausted; but they who wait for the Lord shall renew their strength; they shall mount up with wings like eagles; they shall run and not be weary; they shall walk and not faint.

Do we trust God to help us handle all things, so that we can rest peacefully at night?

____

____

____

Dr. Stacy's Powerful Peaceful prayer

Lord, teach us parents to learn the value in resting and give us strength to usher our families into the peace and tranquility of the night.

Your Powerful Peaceful prayer

____

____

____

Chapter 10

Discipline

For every minute you are angry
you lose sixty seconds of happiness.
Ralph Waldo Emerson

I would be willing to bet that many of my readers will have skipped all the other chapters in this book and have turned directly to this one. There is a specific reason I didn't place this chapter earlier on. It's really important to hear about all the other parenting strategies first. Why? I promise that if you understand and implement the suggestions in Chapters 1 through 9, you will need this chapter less and less each day.

Discipline should be about teaching. Many of us, however, think about discipline only when it comes time to punish a child for bad behavior. Discipline should be taking place all day, every day. The more we discipline—in a healthy, positive way—the less we have to punish. Have you ever looked up the definition of "discipline"? If not, here is the first entry in my dictionary: discipline is "the practice of training people to obey rules or a code of behavior."

Are you training your children to clean their room? Are you training your child to listen in school? Are you training your child to do his homework? To increase compliance, parents need to be in the habit of training their children in the behavior they want to see.

I do not believe in spanking or using any other corporal punishment to discipline children. Children who are beaten will then start hitting other children and, as they get older, other people. I have seen this too many times in clinical practice. Parents will bring in a preschool child in who is getting into serious trouble at school for hitting her fellow students. The first question I will ask: "Is the child being spanked?" More often than not, reluctantly the parents will answer yes and then I will have them complete a thirty-day no-spanking contract. We agree to work together so that they can learn to discipline, teach, and train their child to respond and behave in different ways.

What often happens in these situations is that a child will get frustrated with his peers' behavior and use the same technique that's been used on him—hitting—in order to change the behavior of his peer. It makes total sense. A better way is to use problem-solving skills and teach our children by modeling with our own discipline that we can use words to change behaviors in others.

Handling physical aggression.

We want to make sure that we are not allowing physical aggression on any level in our homes. If and when an act of physical aggression does occur, utilize a time-out immediately.

Parents should utilize time-outs for children under the age of five; find a quiet space away from busy areas within the house. Make sure the children know that they are being taken to a time-out area and have them sit in a particular chair. Time should be added for each incident where they get out of the chair.

If you begin this disciplinary practice when your kids are toddlers, you won't have to be doing it as they get older. Small children are very reluctant to be removed from their parents' sphere of attention, so this is the best time to utilize this strategy.

Teenagers should have privileges removed for physical aggression and a strong message that this will not be tolerated in the home. We need to make sure that safety is always maintained in our homes even when we disagree.

Parents should not utilize restraints or "bear hugs" during aggression as this often escalates children more. As in most residential and group home settings when we have an acting out patient, we will clear the area and allow the patient time to settle. Do not continue with verbal comments as this too will escalate children.

People tend to get hurt even more when we try physical attempts to resolve physically acting out children. When your child is calm, problem solve ways they can release anger in an appropriate way the next time. Teachable moments...

Minimize the use of punishment to increase its effectiveness.

The parent who punishes for everything will lose out when it comes to disciplining her child. Punishment is meant for serious infractions. Don't give a major punishment for a "minor offense"—if you do, then the next "major offense" will need an even bigger punishment. It could become a vicious cycle, and does not bring peace into the home.

Don't threaten punishment.

In my view, many parents threaten too much. Children become immune to idle threats of punishment. If the offense is serious, take immediate action and punish. If the offense is a minor one, then utilize it as a teaching moment, rather than wasting this opportunity by idle threats.

Keep in mind your big goals here. Children need to know what their boundaries are, and while they may not enjoy being corrected, in the end they feel safer. As parents, we want our kids to develop appropriate behavior whether in the home or out in the world

Give privileges instead of taking them away.

I often remind parents that most of what our children have are really privileges—privileges that we gladly give them. Sometimes, a parent will try to discipline his child by taking away fun things or activities. But—referring back to Chapter 2—I feel that praise is a more effective tool.

I suggest you encourage and reinforce the behavior you want to see by giving the "extras" in life as a reward for a great day. Movies, computer time, telephones, etc., are not rights; they're privileges. Instead of continually threatening and then taking away privileges, which only creates a negative relationship, I encourage you to be a giver.

If you must punish, make it consistent.

I have seen parents who sometimes, but not always, punish a child for breaking curfew. This hot-and-cold attitude is a surefire recipe for disaster. Be consistent with what you consider a punishable offense and punish it every time—not just some of the time.

Your consistent response is what will decrease the likelihood of the behavior returning, not the varying degrees of punishment.

Discuss your concerns ahead of time.

I believe that every child should know what acceptable behavior is. For example, don't punish your child for bouncing the ball in the house if you've never taught her where she can, and can't, bounce the ball. Sometimes parents make assumptions about what their kids know concerning family expectations; when the kids haven't had them explained to them, they inevitably fall short, and they're punished. Remember, they're not mind-readers.

Make sure that you discuss these things with your children. Remind them as necessary. For example, when you're just about to go into a restaurant, you can say: "I want to see everyone sitting quietly and using your manners." Let them know what you expect, so it's not a guessing game for anyone.

Keep punishment short.

The forever punishment sounds good in theory but it does not work well with children. Parents who give no indication of when punishment will end are giving forever punishments. Children need to have an end date and time to punishment. It gives them hope and an understanding that they will be back to normal soon.

We do not want children giving up hope because then they'll often stop trying to behave well as they "are punished forever anyway . . . Who cares."

Does this sound familiar in your home? If so, be sure to keep punishments short so that you can be consistent and follow through with them as well. Parents let's face it we are punished when they are punished, so short punishments work for everyone.

Be your own judge.

Many parents try to compare their punishments to how other parents are handling problems, or are confused as to what is disrespectful behavior. I worked in residential programs for five years and so I have an extremely high level of tolerance for smart-mouthed children. I am not as easily swayed by verbal disrespect as another parent may be.

I am very mild-mannered in most problem situations with my kids due to my professional experience in dealing with children in crisis. I have watched parents yell and scream angrily about behaviors that if it were my child, I could easily ignore. Yes, I said ignore. But every home, every family, is different.

You have to think about your child, your home, and your ability to tolerate your children's imperfections. Let's face it—children will make mistakes and we have to be ready for them.

My children have often heard me say, "Mommy does not reward stinky behavior." They know that I always want to have fun with them and to give to them. They also know that I don't always give them want they want and that if they're not behaving, they shouldn't be asking me for privileges. I am a fair parent with my children and I believe that discipline is about being fair. In my view, we as parents should be thinking every day about how we can reward our children—and not just about when to punish their misbehavior.

Peaceful Parenting

Hebrews 12:11

For the moment all discipline seems painful rather than pleasant, but later it yields the peaceful fruit of righteousness to those who have been trained by it.

What discipline have we avoided in our home because it seemed too difficult to deal with? What would be the outcome if we did deal with the problem?

____

____

____

____

Proverbs 12:1

Whoever loves discipline loves knowledge, but he who hates reproof is stupid.

How do we feel about being disciplined by authority in our life, whether it be by our spouse, our supervisor, our pastor?

---

1 Corinthians 9:27

But I discipline my body and keep it under control, lest after preaching to others I myself should be disqualified . . .

How does our behavior in times of discipline impact the child that we are disciplining? What might we need to change about the way we discipline in order to increase compliance?

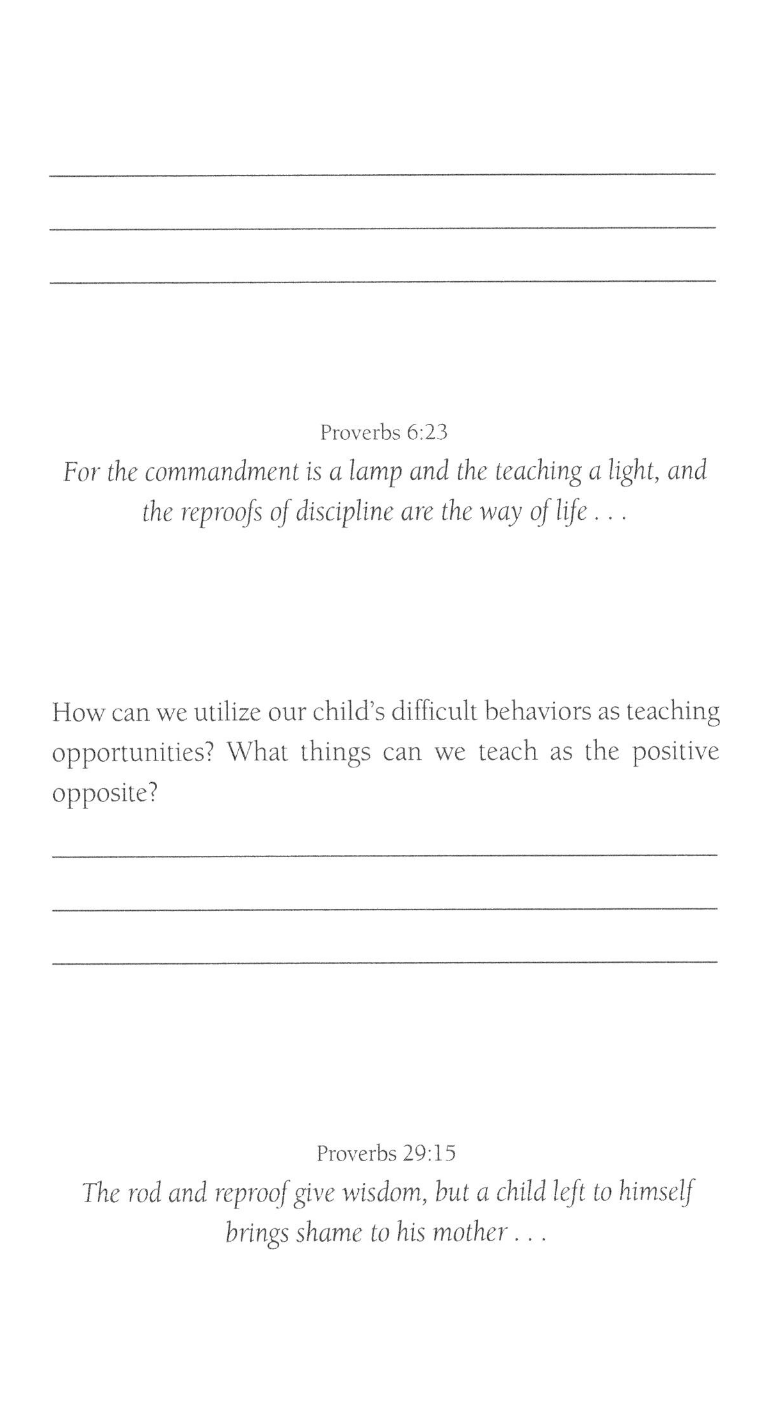

Proverbs 6:23

For the commandment is a lamp and the teaching a light, and the reproofs of discipline are the way of life . . .

How can we utilize our child's difficult behaviors as teaching opportunities? What things can we teach as the positive opposite?

Proverbs 29:15

The rod and reproof give wisdom, but a child left to himself brings shame to his mother . . .

Proverbs 13:24

Whoever spares the rod hates his son, but he who loves him is diligent to discipline him . . .

Many individuals as well as organizations—including some churches—use these verses to justify spanking children. What else do these verses say about changing a child's behavior? What else can we do to discipline our child in a positive way?

____

____

____

Proverbs 29:17

Discipline your son, and he will give you rest; he will give delight to your heart . . .

In what areas do our children not give us delight? How have we actively disciplined them in these areas?

____

____

____

____

Dr. Stacy's Powerful Peaceful prayer

Lord, teach us parents to discipline with love and with wisdom as we are here to guide and direct the destiny of our children.

Your Powerful Peaceful prayer

____

____

____

Chapter 11

Time to Parent

Guard well your spare moments. They are like uncut diamonds. Discard them and their value will never be known. Improve them and they will become the brightest gems in a useful life.

Ralph Waldo Emerson

It seems that no one has time these days. When I talk with teachers they do not have time, when I talk with parents they do not have time. No one has time—which is the one thing our children need most. How is that we have created a life that has no time for the most important thing in our life: our children?

Being busy does not equal spending time and being present with our children. Many children will say that their parents are physically there but that's about it. They're too busy to talk, too busy to listen, too busy to just be present with their family. Parenting takes time and a lot of it.

With children in school six to eight hours a day and

asleep for ten to twelve hours, we really at best only have four to six hours a day to really spend with them. Yet a lot of us are too busy. We have time for work, time for social events, time for friends, time for hobbies, time for church, time for sports, and time for anything else we can busy ourselves with—and yet no time for our children.

Plenty of parents argue that they do spend a majority of their free time with their children and in fact lots of them do. But how much of that time is quality time? How much of the time is spent talking with our children, getting to know them, maybe telling them a funny joke or learning about their new music interest?

Parents of teenagers can get frustrated because when we respond to the pressures to "talk with our teen" they often push us away. With some teenagers, they reject these overtures because they've been trying to spend time and talk with you for years: "So don't try now," as some of these kids will say.

If we're going to see children achieve their fullest potential and accomplish all that we would like them to, it's going to require time: our time, every day, for the rest of their lives

My happiest moments in life are with my children and I hope to pass the love of parenting on to them and to my grandchildren. Thanks Dad for teaching me the simple phrase "I love you and I am proud of you" and for telling me each and every day.

Ecclesiastes 3:1-8

For everything there is a season, and a time for every matter under heaven: a time to be
born, and a time to die; a time to plant, and a time to pluck up what is planted; a time to
kill, and a time to heal; a time to break down, and a time to build up; a time to weep, and a
time to laugh; a time to mourn, and a time to dance; a time to cast away stones, and a time
to gather stones together; a time to embrace, and a time to refrain from embracing;

We have often read this passage of Scripture. How can we apply this to our season as a
parent?

____

____

____

James 4:13-15

Come now, you who say, "Today or tomorrow we will go into such and such a town and spend a year there and trade and make a profit"— yet you do not know what tomorrow will bring. What is your life? For you are a mist that appears for a little time and then vanishes. Instead you ought to say, "If the Lord wills, we will live and do this or that."

We often hear of individuals with their Bucket List, a list of things to do before they die. What are the things we need to do with our children before they grow up and are no longer children?

____

____

____

Psalms 127:3

Behold, children are a heritage from the Lord, the fruit of the womb a reward

How would God say we are treating our "heritage"?

____

____

____

Proverbs 17:6

Grandchildren are the crown of the aged, and the glory of children is their fathers

How will children be valued in generations to come? What will our children learn from us on how to raise their children?

Dr. Stacy's Powerful Peaceful Prayer

Lord, I pray that we as parents will slow down, take the time to enjoy our daily blessing from you, our children.

Your Powerful Peaceful Prayer

____

____

____

It is not the length of life, but the depth.

Ralph Waldo Emerson

Resources

Books

Greene, R. W. (2008). *Lost at school: Why our children with behavioral challenges are falling through the cracks and how we can help them.* New York: Scribner.

Greene, R. W. (2010) *The explosive child. Revised and updated.* New York: Harper Collins Publisher.

Forehand, R., & Long, N. (2002) *Parenting the strong willed child: The clinically proven five-week program for parents of two to six year olds.* New York: McGraw Hill.

Neu, T. W., & Weinfeld, R. (2007). *Helping boys succeed in school: A practical guide for parents and teachers.* Waco, Tx: Prufrock Press Inc.

Sells, S. (2001). Parenting your out-of-control teenager: 7 Steps to restablish authority and reclaim love. New York, New York: St. Martin's Griffin.

Phelan, T. W. (2003). 1-2-3 Magic: Effective discipline for children 2-13. Glen Ellyn, Illinois: Parentmagic, Inc.

Clark, L. (2005). SOS help for parents: A practical guide for handling common everyday behavior problems. Bowling Green, KY: SOS Programs & Parents Press.

Wyckoff, J., & Unell, B.C. (1984). Discipline without shouting or spanking: Practical solutions to the most common preschool behavior problems. New York, NY: Meadowbrook Press.

Websites

www.livesinthebalance.org Dr. Ross Greene, Collaborative & Proactive Solutions, problem solving approach

www.focusonthefamily.com Dr. James Dobson, Christian advice on marriage, families and other topics.

Dr. Haynes Resources

Weekly Radio Show Parenting Tips 2 Go w/ Dr. Stacy 1360 AM WNJCRadio.com Tuesdays 10am EST

www.parentingtips2go.com Dr. Stacy Haynes, offers tips, parenting webinars, and advice for busy parents

www.littlehandsservices.com Dr. Stacy Haynes, official site for counseling, parent workshops, and continuing education

CPSIA information can be obtained
at www.ICGtesting.com
Printed in the USA
BVHW04s1910120418
513240BV00008B/260/P